100 GEOR

Dick Irwin

Illustrated by Rich
Cover illustration is from an image by Ronald Embleton

100 Geordie Jokes by Dick Irwin. This reprint 2010.

ISBN-13 978-0-946928-29-3
ISBN-10 0-946928-29-0
First published by published by Frank Graham. Published by Butler Publishing in 1988.
©1988 Butler Publishing, Thropton, Morpeth, Northumberland NE65 7LP

BUTLER
publishing

A number of years ago the well known Tyneside comedian, Dick Irwin, was asked to compile a comprehensive collection of his Geordie jokes. From these one hundred have been selected for this book. These jokes are a representative selection and give the reader a good idea of the kind of jokes popular in the music halls and clubs in the middle of the 20th century. They have not been modernized but are presented in the form in which they have delighted thousands of Geordies over the years. In that sense they are not only local jokes but an historic collection and in years to come, even if changes in taste take place, the present book will no doubt still delight its readers and perhaps provide material for the social historian.

1 The V.I.P.s

Geordie and his marra Tucker Johnston had a big win on the pools. So they decided to go on a world cruise. After a week at sea, the Captain called the purser in his cabin to ask what influential people were on board, so he could invite them to his table. "Sir," said the purser, "we have four film stars, three M.P.s and two strange gentlemen from the north, who seem to be very wealthy." The Captain bade him to go round with the invitations. Knocking on Geordie's cabin door, he was greeted by "Howay in bonny lad". When he entered, there was Geordie and Tucker, feet on the table, four bottles of Brown Ale, eating fish and chips. The purser saluted, "Begging your pardon gentlemen," he said, "the Captains compliments, he requests your company at his table tonight." "Ye must be joking!" says Geordie. "Ye divvent think Tucker's and me's gan te spend aal this money to eat with the bloody crew."

2 David Nixon at Club

Ashington Universal Social Club booked magician David Nixon to entertain its aged members Christmas treat. He was pulling fingers out of gloves, feet out of socks, cigarettes out of packets, matches out of matchboxes, etc. At the end of his act he says to Geordie, "Did you enjoy my act Geordie?" "By hinney! Aa did an aal," says Geordie. "Ye'd gan a bomb at the Jolly Boys some Sunday morning, 30 shillings and your beor." "Then," said David Nixon, "would you be surprised if I put my hand in your jacket pocket and pulled a rabbit out?" "I waald an aal," says Geordie, "I've got a ferret in there!"

3 Crocodile Shoes

One night Geordie was having a pint in the club, when he seen a fellow with a very unusual pair of shoes on. Geordie couldn't keep his eyes off them. So he says to the bloke, "How mistor! Whatha kind of shoes is them ye hev on? I'd like to hev a pair of them." "Why," says the gent, "they are crocodile shoes." "Why lad," says Geordie, "I must be thick in the heed but what's a crocodile?" "Well," says the gent, "a crocodile is a reptile, which inhabits the rivers of Africa, the River Zambesi is full of them." "Thanks mistor," says Geordie, "I'll hev te hev a pair of them shoes." So he saved two weeks pay at the pit and books a plane to Africa. Paddling his canoe up the Zambesi, he sees a huge crocodile. Geordie being a big powerful fellow strips off, just a loin cloth, knife between his teeth. Swims to the croc., fights it, kills it, drags it ashore, looks at it and says, "By gox! Eftor all that trouble it's got ne shoes on".

4 Geordie in American Pit

The pit where Geordie worked was made redundant and Geordie lost his job. Reading the papers one day, he sees an advert: Miners wanted in Pennsylvania, U.S.A., £100 a week, house and car supplied. So, fastening his furniture on the tail of a kite he emigrates to U.S.A. First day at the pit, going down in the cage, the cage stops. Geordie says to an American, "How lad, is this where we start work, is this the coal fyce?" "Say are you the guy from England?" says the Yank. "I'm from Backworth son," says Geordie. "Waal Bud! you don't start here, you wait here, a lil old diesel train comes along, you git on, you have a two and a half hours ride." Why Geordie has the two and a half hours ride. Says to the Yank, "De we myke a start noo hinney?" "No Bud," says the Yank, "you stand here, another train comes, you have another two hours ride." This goes on all day, 8 o'clock in the morning till 5 p.m. at night. Geordie nivor struck a bat. He couldn't stand no more. "Bonny Lad," he says to the Yank, "I've had enough of this, its worse than working, I'm gannin back hyem the morn." "Gee Geordie," says the Yank, "you can't leave us now, we are at war with Vietnam!" "Ye've a bloody good reet," says Geordie, "ye're pinchin thor coal!"

5 Leek Pudding

Geordie comes in from the pit after a hard shift. His wife had a leek pudding on the table for him. Geordie looks at it. "By gox!" he says, "That's a big leek pudding it'll be for wor Jimmy." "No," she says, "it's not for wor Jimmy." "By it's the biggest leek pudding I've seen," says Geordie. "A knaa then it's for wor Tommy." "No," she says, "it's not for wor Tommy." "Mind its a monster," says Geordie. "I bet it's for wor Willie." "You're wrang," she says, "it's not for wor Willie." "Why lass whe's it for," says

Geordie, "cos it's sartinly a big un?" "Why," she says, "if ye must knaa it's for ye." "Blimey," says Geordie, "what a little un!"

6 What's in a name?

I remember gannin to watch Newcastle United playing Rangers at St. James. It was like being in Belfast. Beer bottles flying aboot like machine gun bullets, a little fellow in front of me was dookin and dodging. I says, "It's ne good ye dein that lad, if one of them bottles has your name on ye'll get it." "Thats whit I'm worried aboot sorr," he says, "they call me McEwan!"

7 Geordie on T.V.

Geordie went to Newcastle with his wife to do a bit shopping, while she was shopping he wandered into Tyne Tees Studio and took part in a quiz, to his delight he won first prize. Quiz master says, "You have won first prize, you can have a piano or a pianola." "Why what's the difference?" says Geordie. "Well," says the quiz master, "to play the piano you have to be a musician, but anyone can use the pianola." "I'll tyeke the pianola," says Geordie. When he got home the whole family is there to greet him. "We seen you on the telly, what did you get?" says his father. "Why I could have had a piano or a pianola," says Geordie, "so I choose the pianola." "What for?" says the old man. "Why," says Geordie, "ye've got to be a musician to play the piano, but anybody can use the pianola, I can use it, the wife can use it, the bairns can use it, ye can use it." His old mother looked up from her knitting, "Aye," she says, "but I knaa who'll hev to empty it!"

8 Ask a Daft Question

One day when Geordie was doon the toon, he sees a greet big funeral coming up the Haymarket. Brass band, four plumed horses pulling the hearse, six coaches and aboot 2,000 mourners in silk hats waalking ahint. By gox! he thinks, he must be an important bloke. That must be a Lord Mayor or Chief of Police or something. I'll just ax this paper lad, he'll knaa whe it is. "Son," says Geordie, "d'ye knaa whe it is that's deed ower thonder?" "Ee I'm not sure," says the paper lad, "but I think its that bloke in the forst carriage."

9 Heavenly Telephone

Geordie's brother Jonty passed away. Geordie bought a little wooden cross to put on Jonty's grave. When he went to put some flowers on the grave he discovered the wind had blown the cross to the right, so he straightened it up and put a wooden chock in. Next day he went down, the wind had blown the cross to the left. He thought, what am I ganna de noo? He saw a coil of wire lying on the ground. The Redifussion lads had been working there. So he got a wonderful idea. He fastened one end of the wire on the cross, and the other end on the highest branch of a nearby tree. That night he went to the club for a pint. His mate Tucker says, "Geordie, I see your Jonty's deein weel since he snuffed it." "How that?" says Geordie. "Why," says Tucker, "I passed his grave this morning, I see he's got the telephone in noo!"

10 Faith Healer

A famous faith healer had been to Newbiggin Welfare Hall. The following night Geordie and Tucker were having a talk in the Club. Tucker says, "I took wor little Jimmy doon te see him, ye knaa wor Jimmy wi the crutches?" "Gaan on," says Geordie, "what happened?" "Why he says te wor Jimmy, 'Stand there, son, I'll sing a hymn, say a prayer, then I want you to throw away your left crutch'. So he sang a hymn and said a prayer." "Aye, gaan on," says Geordie, "what happened then?" "Why," says Tucker, "wor Jimmy straightened himsel' up, took a breath and hoyed away his left crutch." "Gaan on," says Geordie. "Why," says Tucker, "the faith healer says to wor Jimmy, 'I'll sing another hymn, say a prayer then you will cast away your right crutch'. So he sang another hymn, said a prayer and then..." "Gaan on, man," says Geordie, "what did Jimmy de then?" "Why," says Tucker, "Jimmy straightened up raised his eyes to heaven, then threw away his right crutch." "Did he waalk?" says Geordie. "Did he hell," says Tucker, "he fell flat on his back!"

11 Claes Prop

Geordie's wife bought a claes prop off a man in the lane just to discover that there was no V in the top. So she couldn't hang the clothes out. When Geordie came in from the pit she told him about it. "Divvent worry," he says, "as soon as I've had me dinner I'll git the saw oot the tool box and I'll hev a V sawn in yor prop afore ye can say Jack Robinson." He gets the saw oot the box, gaans tiv his next door neighbour Tucker Johnson. "Tucker," he says, "can ye lend us your extension ladder?" "Sartinly," says Tucker, "Are ye ganna paint yor ootside?" "No," says Geordie, "the wife's bowt a prop with ne V in the top and I want te climb up the ladder and saw a V in it." "Ye must be barmy," says Tucker, "ye divvent need ne ladder te saw a V in a prop. De what I de, gaan hyem, dig a hole in the garden, stick the prop in, gaan upstairs, lean oot the bedroom window and saw a V in."

12 A Helping Hand

It was a cold frosty night, Geordie noticed this Salvation Army lass standing outside the pub holding a banner bearing the slogan, Down with the Demon Drink. Geordie says to her, "Hinney, you look frozen, your nose is as reed as a chorry, would you like a glass of whisky to waarm ye up?" "How dare you even suggest that sir," she said. "I couldn't stand out here drinking whisky and holding this banner." "I wasn't being cheeky hinney," says Geordie, "I was only trying to help ye, I could fetch it oot in a teacup, nebody would knaa. They would think ye were supping tea." She thought a while then said, "Go on then, I'll risk it". Geordie gaans in the pub, says te the landlord, "Henna, give us a pint hinney and put a large whisky in a teacup". "Good God," said the landlord, "is that Salvation Army lass oot there agyen?"

13 Feed Thy Flock

Geordie's wife invited the minister to dinner. Geordie, who kept hens, killed two chickens for the occasion. The minister wolfed the lot bones and all. After the meal Geordie was showing the minister round his small holding, an old rooster was sitting on the gate-post crowing his head off. "My," says the minister, "that bird sounds proud of himself." "He's got a bloody good reet," says Geordie, "he's got two sons in the ministry."

14 Oh Father

Geordie was in the club Sunday morning. After drinking 10 bottles of 'brown', 7 pints of beer, 3 whiskys, I rum, he fell flat on his back. The barman says, "That's what I like aboot Geordie, knaas when he's had enough." On the way hyem he meets a priest. He looks at the priest and says, "D'ye knaa your collars on the wrang way roond?" "Naturally my son," says the priest, "I'm a father." "That's nowt," says Geordie, "I'm the fethor of ten and I've got ne collar on, just an aald muffler." "You don't understand," said the priest, "I happen to be the father of millions." "You should think a thousand shyems," says Geordie, "standing there on a Sunday morning taalking like that, man its not your collar ye want turning roond, it's yor linings."

15 Seeing is Believing
Geordie had had too much to drink. 12 o' clock at night he's trying to open the front door with a chip. The pollis gets his eye on him, being a sergeant and well trained he puts two and two together. "That man's drunk," he says. "Noo my man, what's gannin on heor?" "It's alreet Mr. Pollis," says Geordie. "I'm not a burglar, it's my hoose, paid for, I owe ne-body nowt." He takes the pollis in. Gives him a drink out the frig, "Awl paid for, I owe ne-body nowt". Shows the pollis the whole house, stressing the fact everything was paid for. Finishing up in the bedroom he says to the pollis: "D'ye see that maaogany wardrobe, oak dressing table, aal mine, aal paid for, and ye see that double bed, that's mine anaal and ye see that woman lying in bed, that's my wife, and ye see that bloke lying aside her, that's me."

16 German Midget
The London to Edinburgh Express was standing in Kings Cross, in one carriage sat a braw Scot, 6 ft. 3 ins., kilt, sporran, tam-o-shanter, the lot. A little German midget got in the same carriage. "Ooh ma wee man where are ye off tae the noo?" says the Scot. "Ach mein freund," says the wee German, "I'm to Newcastle-on-der-Tyne going, where I vas in der circus of der Bertram Mills, ya." "Ye'll be lucky," says Jock, "the train doesna stop at Newcastle, 300 mile an hour from here tae Scotland. But I'll tell ye what I'll do, when the train gets to Newcastle it slows doon tae 100 mile an hour. I'll wind the window doon, grab ye by the scruff o' your neck, drop ye on the platform, and ye can make your way from then." "Danke mein Herr," said wee Hans. All went well, the train slowed down to 100 m.p.h. at Central Station, Jock dropped the German midget out. Away he went like a shot oot of a gun. Just as he got to the guards van, the guard leaned out of the van picked him up, hoyed him back on the train, saying, "Anybody that can run as fast as that deserves to catch the train".

17 Resurrection Day
Geordie's wife was getting worried about his excessive drinking. So she went to the Doctor for advice. "There's only one cure," said the Doctor. "Take him out one night, get him good and drunk, then give him the biggest fright he ever had in his life, that'll finish him with the drink." So she took him oot one Saturday night, she started at the top of Scotswood Road and finished up in Leadgate, took him in every pub on

the road. Filled him full of beer, whisky, rum, lemonade and caald tea and got him as drunk as a monkey. On the way home, they had to walk through a churchyard, and there was an empty grave. Being a dark night she sat Geordie in the grave, thinking when he wakes up in the morning he'll get the biggest fright in his life. But what a mistake, when Geordie woke the next day it was a lovely sunny day. Geordie climbed out the grave, pulled the soil out his hair, saw all the headstones, crossed himself, saying, "By gox, Resurrection Day already and I'm the forst un up".

18 Fatherly Advice

Geordie's reading the paper one night, when he turned to his wife Meggie. "Can ye mind thon vicar that married us thirty year ago, why I'm reading here, he wasn't a vicar at aal, he's an impostor, spurious. That means after thirty years of happy married life, we are not even married, I'm still a bachelor." "Good God," she says, "I'll still be a spinster." "Anarnd se," says Geordie. The little laddie was having his dinner. He looked up, and said, "What does that make me fethor?" "Divvent worry son," says Geordie, "ye aalways wanted to be a pollis didn't ye?"

19 Buttonholes

Geordie had a plague of black-beetles in his colliery house. Telling his mate at work about it, his mate says, "There's only one cure, flowers! Any sort, daisies, roses, pansies. Scatter them on the mat. Ye'll soon get rid of your beetles." At the weekend, Geordie and his mate met in the pub. "By the way," says his mate, "did ye try me cure?" "I did an aal," says Geordie. "I got dozens of flooers, aal sorts, hoyed them aal ower the floor." "And did it get rid of the beetles?" says his mate. "Did it hell," says Geordie, "they're running aboot with buttonholes in noo."

20 Hev a Blaw

Geordie had been oot in his new car, one previous owner, Julius Caesar. Two tone black and rust. Coming hyem it was a dark foggy night. Couldn't see a hand in front of you, when the panda car pulls Geordie up. Oot steps the pollis, "Excuse me sir would you mind blowing in that?" Geordie couldn't see nowt so he blew. "Would you mind blowing again sir?" says the pollis. So Geordie blaws again. "Thank you sir," says the pollis, "I hate putting these gloves on on a caald neet."

21 Riding Boots

It was Saturday neet in the Shakespeare. A bloke walked in the bar with a brown
paper parcel under his arm. "Could I have a pint on tick?" he asks the landlord.
"Sorry, ne tick heor," says the landlord. "I'll tell what," says the stranger, "I've got a
pair of riding boots in this parcel, give us ten bob and they're yours." The landlord
thinks I've always fancied a pair of riding boots. "Okay here's your ten bob." Five
minutes later, he thinks, I'll just have a look at these riding boots. When he opened
the parcel here's a pair of old boots, all holes, worn, down at heel, beyond repair.
Dashing up the road, he found the bloke who sold him them, in a pub up the road. "I
want te see ye, lad. I thowt ye said these were riding boots." "Sartinly they are," says
the bloke, "hev ye tried waalkin in them?"

22 Fair Exchange

Geordie was at Bedlington for the Picnic. He thowt he would caal and see his aald marra, Sammy Bradley. He knocked at the door, Sam's wife opened it. "Noo, Mary," says Geordie, "I've caaled to see Sam." "Hev ye not hord, Geordie," she says, "Sam's deed. He's still upstairs, if ye want te gaan and hev a look at him." Why Geordie gaans upstairs, here's Sam lying deed as a haddock, laughing all ower his fyce, must hev died in his sleep, didn't knaa he was deed and he must hev died wiv his eyes open, cos Mary had put two half-crowns in. Geordie thinks, what a shyem, two bottles of Broon gannin for a burton. So he removed the two silver coins, replacing them with two copper ones. When he went downstairs Mary says, "Did ye see him Geordie?" Geordie says, "I did an aal." "How d'ye think he looks?" she says. "Champion," says Geordie. "Did ye see any change in him?" says Mary. "Aye," says Geordie, "four and tenpence."

23 Keep Yor Heed

Geordie had bought himself a brand new motor-bike. He says tiv his marra, "Tucker, would ye fancy a ride on the back of me bike?" Why Tucker's on the back. Geordies doing about 70 m.p.h. when Tucker shouts, "Geordie, Stop! It's the wind, it's cutting the chest oot of us". Geordie pulls up, says, "I'll tell ye what, take your jacket off, put it on back te front, it'll keep yor chest warm." So Tucker takes his jacket off, puts it on back to front. About three miles further on Geordie turns to Tucker to see if he was alright. No Tucker! He'd fallen off! Geordie turned round. So far along the road he saw a crowd of men with Tucker lying on the road. Geordie dashes up saying, "That's me marra, he's fallen off me bike, is he alreet?" One fellow says, "Why, he was alreet when we found him, but he hasn't spoken a word since we turned his head the right way round."

24 Freedom

The Labour candidate for Swalwell was standing on his soap box on the Town Moor. He spoke: "Comrades, it behoves every one here today to vote Labour. And why? Because when Labour is in power you will get freedom, a thing you never got under Tory rule." He picked one man in the crowd. "You sir, do you see that Rolls Royce over on the road? Vote Labour, get freedom in the land and we will see you get a Rolls like that." Thunderous applause. Then he turned to another man. "You sir, look at your clothes, shabby, worn, threadbare, vote Labour, get freedom in the land, and we will see you wearing Bond Street suits." More applause. Then he pointed to a little man, saying nowt. "You!" he thundered, "Vote Labour, get freedom in the land and you wont be smoking your filthy cigarettes, you will be smoking cigars and the same brand as Mr. Churchill, we will see to it when freedom comes." "Sounds very nice," said the little fellow, "but I don't smoke." The candidate glowered at him. "You'll do what you're told, when freedom comes," he said.

25 Two on a Bike

There was no love lost between the vicar and the pollis in Stakeford. The pollis tried all ways to catch the vicar, with no success, till one day he was on point duty when the vicar came braying doon the High Street on his cycle. When the pollis put his hand up to stop, the vicar, with a squeal of brakes, just pulled up in time. "Nearly got you that time Vicar," says the pollis. "Constable," says the vicar, "you'll never catch me, God is with me you see, God is with me." "Ah! Got you this time Vicar," says the pollis, "two on a bike!"

26 Geordie's Big Leak Show

The American in the bar was boasting about all the wonderful things they had in the U.S.A. Geordie got fed up, he says to the Yank, "Sup up son, come wi me and I'll show you two of the best continents in Europe, Newcastle and Gatesheed." They got on a bus at the Haymarket, the Yank gets his eye on the Civic Centre, shouts of the conductor, "Say, what's that lil ol telephone kiosk over there?" "What d'ye mean?" says the conductor, a true blue Byker lad. "I'll hev ye knaa that's wor Civic Centre, the pride of Geordieland, Dan's Castle." "Gee I'm sorry," said the Yank, "we have telephone kiosks like that in America." Just then they crossed the High Level Bridge, the Yank stuck his head out the Gateshead side and looked at the Tyne, shouted of the conductor, "Say conductor what's that lil ol trickle of water down there?" The conductor looked at the Tyne, shouted to the driver, "Mohammed hinney, pull up, the radiators leaking again".

27 That's the Spirit

Maggie Johnson had just lost her man, Tom, and was grieving. Hor next door neighbour Sally Lunn says, "Why divvent ye come with me to the spuggie meeting your Tom'll taalk to ye." "D'ye think se?" says Maggie. "I knaa see," says Sally, "tho they divvent all come back as humans, my man's a bull in Spain." So Meggie goes to the seance. The medium went into a trance. "Have I a Mrs. Johnson in the congregation, your husband Tom wants to speak to you?" A voice came over the trumpet. "Is that ye Meggie? This is Tom." "Tom it's lovely to hear ye pet," says Maggie, "are you happy?" "I've nivvor been se happy afore," says Tom, "it's one long life of love here, love in the morning, noon and neet." "Oh I am glad," says Maggie. "Are ye an angel in Heaven?" "Am I hell," says Tom, "I'm a rabbit in Plessey Woods!"

rich

15

28 One to Cap the Lot

Little Tadger came in from school crying. "Ma!" he says, "Aal me mates at school keep caaling me big heed, hevn't I not got a big heed Ma?" "Of course ye haven't got a big heed son," said his mother. "Just nip doon te the corner shop and get me three stone of taties... in yor cap."

29 Geordie the Film Critic

Geordie and Tucker were discussing films. Tucker says, "Ye shud gaan te the Roxy the neet, there's a grand pictor on - Moby Dick." "I divvent think I'll bother," says Geordie, "I care nowt for them sex pictors." "Divvent be daft," says Tucker, "it's nowt te de with sex, it's aal aboot whales." "I divvent like Welsh pictors either," says Geordie.

30 Better Safe Than Sorry

Geordie was always getting drunk, and when he came home Maggie, his wife, would lay into him and knock him black and blue. With no avail, so she went to see the doctor. The doctor said, "Why don't you try kindness for a change, it may have the desired effect?" Why the next night Geordie came rolling in palatic. Maggie sat him in the armchair took off his shoes, warmed his slippers, put them on, gave him a bottle of Broon and a sandwich and filled his pipe. After he'd had a smoke she says, "Now darling, would you like te gan te bed noo?" "Aye, we might as weel," says Geordie, "the wife'll only murder us if I gaan hyem."

31 Saint Geordie Meets The Dragon

Geordie went in this old fashioned pub, called the George and Dragon. The land-lady of the George and Dragon was behind the counter, a face like a bag of chisels, 181 stone with her eyebrows plucked, and her ears pierced.
She looked at Geordie in a loud voice, saying, "I hope ye divvent tender a pund note for a gill of beor, and divvent stand ower near the gas fire". "Excuse me missis," says Geordie, "can I hev a word with George?"

32 Batman Geordie

During his army career, Geordie was made Batman to a fiery old major. The major explained to Geordie, "You have a simple duty my man, all you do is waken me at 7 a.m. each morning with a cup of tea, saying good morning sir, nice morning sir, 7 o'clock sir, and a nice cup or tea sir." Well the first morning Geordie wakens him up. "Good morning sir, nice morning sir, 7 o'clock sir, and a nice cup of tea sir." Second and third morning, the same thing. After a week of this Geordie was fed up. On the

Monday morning he went in the major's tent. "Good morning sir, nice morning sir, 7 o'clock sir, and a nice cup of tea sir." "I know, I know!" said the major. "Get out!" "Why ye divvent knaa," says Geordie, "it's 9.30, its raining like hell and it's cocoa."

33 Pride Comes Before the Fall

Geordie met old Jimmy Turnbull coming down the street. "Why Jim," he says, "I'm glad to see ye, hev ye been bad?" "No Geordie," says aald Jim, "I've been in jail." "Jail!" says Geordie, "What's an aald man like ye been deein in jail?" "Why," says old Jim, "I was coming hyem one day, minding me aan business, when a young pollis stopped me, 'Would ye like to help me oot Dad,' he says, 'we're one man short on an identifacin parade'. Why I had nowt te de so I went. Why they stood me in a row with aboot other 10 blokes, shone big spotlights on us, then a young lass in a mini skirt walked in. She bent doon te pick a tab end up, I saw her shoulder blades, she walked alang the parade stopped in front of me pointed at me and said, 'That's him, that's the dorty aald man who attacked me in a back lane'. Why Geordie hinney I was that proud, I pleaded guilty."

34 Fairs Fair

Geordie and Tucker won £3,000 on the pools between them. They were out celebrating in the pub. Tucker says, "D'ye fancy a pie Geordie?" "Aye," says Geordie. So Tucker buys two pies. Further down the street they were looking in a car showroom. Geordie says, "Ye knaa Tucker, we're mugs waalking wi aal this money, we should hev a car apiece." They went in the showroom, Tucker says to the salesman, "How much are them two Jags hinney?" "£1,500 each sir," said the salesman. "Champion," says Tucker, "I'll take the two of them." "Ye'll de nowt of the sort," says Geordie, "ye'll keep yor hand in your pocket, I'll pay for them, ye paid for the pies."

35 Speak When You're Spoken To

One Saturday night Geordie came in well served from the local carrying a duck under his arm. Giving his wife a kiss, he says to her, "What d'ye think of this pig hinney?" "Divvent be se fond," she says, "ye're drunk agyen, that's not a pig, it's a duck." "I'm not taalking te ye," says Geordie, "I'm taalking te the duck."

36 Seeing Double

A bloke came in the bar. The barman says, "What'll you have sir?" "I'll have a double whisky," says the gent. The barman served him saying, "That'll be 60p sir." "I'm paying nowt," says the bloke. "You asked me what I'd have, and I said I'll have a double whisky." A gentleman standing by said to the barman, "I am a barrister, and I'm afraid this man is within his rights, you see your approach was wrong, you should have said, 'What is your order?' or 'What can I serve you with?'." "Okay," says the barman, "I'll admit I've been taken for a ride." He said to the bloke, "Drink your whisky, get out of this pub, and don't show your face in here again, ever!" Half an hour later, the same character walked in the pub. The barman said, "Look you! I told you to stay out of here!" "What de ye mean," says the bloke, "I've nivor been in this pub in my life before." "Good God," says the manager, "you must have a double." "Yes please," says the bloke, "a double whisky."

37 Take It or Leave It

Geordie took Maggie to Spain on a holiday to a big posh hotel. At the end of the holiday he went to the manager and gave him a fiver. "Gracias Senor," said the manager, "you are very kind. Now Senor about your bill, £100." "£100 pond for two weeks, ye must be joking," says Geordie, "ye've had it." "Senor! There was £30 for wines." "I nivor had it," says Geordie. "Perhaps Senor, but it was there if you wanted it," said the manager. "And Senor, £20 for the use of the swimming pool." "I nivor used that either," says Geordie. "It was there if you wanted it, Senor," says the manager. "Right!" says Geordie, "Ye owe me £500 for interfering with wor lass." "Senor," said the manager, "I never touched your wife." "No?" says Geordie, "I divvent knaa aboot that, but she was there if ye wanted te, wasn't she?"

38 Whe's This Billy Graham?

There was these two Geordies arguing about religion. One says tiv his mate, "I knaa The Bible inside oot. I knaa The Book of Moses, The Book of Isaiah, one eye's 'igher than tother, I knaa the whole Bible." His mate says, "Look I went to scyul wi ye and if I can hoy my mind back I divvent think ye ivor went to Sunday scyul. If ye can say the Lords Prayer withoot one mistake I'll give ye a fiver." His mate says, "You're on, here goes. The Lords Prayer.

> Our Father which art in Heaven,
> Hark the Herald Angels sing,
> O God our help in ages past,
> Heaven help the sailors on a night like this.
> AMEN."

His mate says, "Aye yor reet, there's yor fiver, I did'ot think ye knew it."

39 The Seat of Larnin

An argument cropped up in the pit canteen between Geordie and Tucker about Singapore. Geordie says, "It belangs to the Japs." Tucker says, "I think it belangs to us." After an hours discussion they couldn't make their minds up. So Geordie says, "We're gittin ne where fast, let's axe the deputy, he's an educated man, he's boond te knaa." So Geordie pulls the deputy up. "Waald ye settle an argument?" he says. "Tucker says Singapore belangs te the Japs, I say it belangs to us, could ye settle the argument and tell us whe it belangs te?" The deputy looked thoughtful then said, "Why lads I'm not sure whe it belangs te but I'm varny sure Jarvis trains it."

40 Ye Live and Larn

Geordie was watching a speaker in the Bigg Market decrying the evils of strong drink. "I have here a glass of water and also a glass of whisky. I take an ordinary earth worm, drop it in the water and it swims merrily around. I take it out of the water drop it in the glass of whisky and lo and behold it shrivels up and dies. Now I hope this demonstration has learned someone in my audience a lesson." Geordie says, "It sartinly larned me a lesson sir, I knaa noo, if you've got worms drink whisky."

41 Fine Feathers Make Flat Birds

Old Mrs. Turnbull went in the grocer's. "Could I hev a packet of Daz, to wash me budgie in?" she says. "Hinney," says the grocer, "I waadn't recommend it, it's a varry powerful detergent and might kill yor budgie." "Nowt of the sort," says Mrs. Turnbull. "The wife next door weshes her budgie regular in Daz, and it comes up lovely."

"Alreet," says the grocer, "It's yor idea, divvent hold me responsible if owt happens." Three weeks later Mrs. Turnbull came in the shop. "How is yor budgie?" says the grocer. "Oh hinney, it's deed," she says. "I towld ye the Daz would kill it," says the grocer. "Oh it wasn't the Daz," says Mrs. Turnbull, "it was when I put it through the mangle."

42 When Did You Last See Your Father?

Young Bantie Johnson joined H.M. Royal Navy. One day walking along a street in Hong Kong he saw a parrot in a cage. The parrot looked at him and said, "Wot cheor Kiddar, I knaa ye." "By gox," thinks young Bantie, "a parrot that taalks Geordie, I'll buy it for me muther, she'll be ower the moon with that." He goes in the shop, says to the old Chinaman behind the counter, "How much d'ye want for that parrot hinney, it taalks my language?" "Velly solly," says the old Chinaman, "pallot not for sale, but I have egg flom pallot £5." "Okay," says Bantie, "I'll take the egg." Three years later he's in Hong Kong again, same street, same shop, same parrot. The parrot looks at him and says, "Wot cheor Kiddar, I knaa ye." "Aye," says Bantie, "I knaa ye an all, yer fethor was a duck."

43 Keep Death Off The Road

Geordie was asking Tucker where he was thinking of going on his holidays. Tucker says, "I fancy gannin to France." "Will ye be taking yor car?" says Geordie. "Oh aye," says Tucker, "I'll be taking the wife and bairns for a run." "Be careful," says Geordie, "cos them continentals are not like us, they drive on the right side of the road, not the left." "Thanks," says Tucker, "I'll remember that." A week later Geordie's walking up the lane, here's Tucker knocking the dents out of his mudguards, straightening the headlamps. "Wot cheor marra," says Geordie, "hev you had an accident?" "No," says Tucker, "but I've changed my mind, I'm not gannin to France now. I had a bit practice on Northumberland Street. It's dangerous."

44 Speak For Yersel

Geordie got a job as a coalman. One day passing the high rise flats in Walker, he heard a voice from the 15th floor ordering 10 bags of coal. When he got inside the lift was broken, so he had to carry each bag up separately. After he put all bags in the coalhouse he knocked at the front door, "That'll be £10 madam for 10 bags of coal," he said to the housewife. "What are ye taalking aboot?" she says, "I ordered ne coal." "I distinctly heard the voice oot the window saying ten bags please," says Geordie, "and I've carried them upstairs." "Good God," she says, "it'll be that parrot." So she paid him. When her man came in from work that night she told him about the parrot ordering the coal. Her man went mad, "I'll morder it!" he yells. He took the parrot out of the cage, swung it around and hoyed it in the corner. As he was doing this he tripped over the cat so he kicked the cat, the cat landed beside the parrot. The parrot opened one eye, looked at the cat and said, "How many bags did ye order mate?"

45 The Chain Gang

I remember my first car, one previous owner, Julius Caesar, two tone, black and rust. One night it broke down in Chester-le-Street. I was trying to start it when an old Durham pitman (canny lads) passed. "Is thou having trouble son?" he says. "Actually piston broke," I told him. "Nivor mind, so am I," he says. "But divvent worry son, nobody gets stranded here, thou can come and bide wi me for the neet and I want ne money, if thou offers me any money I'll be insulted. Thou can give the 27 bairns 50p each, but I want ne money." He was as good as his word, he took me to his colliery house, the fire was blazing, gave me a lovely supper, pies and peas, and the 27 bairns sang Blow the Wind Southerly. Then he says, "If you want to use the netty it's doon the garden." When I came back he says, "Did thou find it?" "Yes thanks,"

I said. "Did thou pull the chine?" "Yes," I said. "I thowt se," he says, "ye've let all the pigeons oot."

46 Down By The Riverside
The anti-drink evangelist was standing on his soap box on the quayside. "My friends," he said, "all alcohol should be done away with, every barrel of beer, every bottle of whisky, rum, gin and brandy should be seized and cast into the Tyne. My friends let us all join in and sing hymn four hundred and fowerty-fower—*Shall We Gather by the River.*"

47 What's in a Name?

Geordie's daughter Dorothy had just presented him with a little grandson. "What should I caal him dad?" she says. "Why," says Geordie, "caal him a good biblical name, ye canna whack a name oot The Bible. Caal him Harald." "Why dad," she says, "there's ne Harald in the Bible!" "Why sartinly there is," says Geordie, "hev ye nivor hord of Hark the Harald Angels Sing?"

48 Geordie and the Big Flood

Geordie was down on his luck, he applied to a circus on the Town Moor for a job. The boss said, "We've got a job that'll just suit you, washing the elephant. Now it's an easy job. The elephants name is Nuts, when you wash his back, you say, 'Down Nuts', he will kneel down. When you want to wash underneath you say, 'Up Nuts', then he will stand up." "Sounds alreet te me," says Geordie, "I'll take the job." Well an hour later Geordie dashes in to the boss's caravan, soaking wet. "I'm packing in," he says, "I want me cards." "Why, what's wrong?" says the boss. "Well," Geordie says, "the job was gannin champion, I said, 'Down Nuts', he knelt down, I washed his back. Then I said, 'Up Nuts', and he stood up. I'd just started washing underneath when a fellow with a tray passed shouting, 'Pea Nuts'."

49 Famous Last Words

Geordie bought a budgie with a nice cage. After a week the budgie hadn't spoke a word. Geordie went back to the shop, "That budgie hasn't spoken," he said to the shopkeeper. "Perhaps it's lonely, has it got a mirror?" "No," says Geordie, and buys a mirror. Another week went by without the bird speaking, back goes Geordie to the shop. "Try buying it a little bell and a ladder," says the shopkeeper. So Geordie buys a bell and a ladder. Three weeks later Geordie walks in the shop. "Good morning sir," says the shopkeeper, "How's your budgie?" "Oh," says Geordie, "I've caaled to tell ye it's deed." "Oh I am sorry," said the shopkeeper, "did it ever speak?" "Oh aye," says Geordie, "just before it dropped doon deed it said, 'Geordie does that shop not sell bird seed?'."

50 Double-Blank

Geordie walked into a pub in the country village of Wooler. After two pints he happened to look round, sitting at a table was an old shepherd playing dominoes with a collie dog. By gox, it must be strong beor heor, he thought.
He went over to the table and watched them play another two games, then
he said to the shepherd, "By that's a clivver dog you've got there, I've nivor seen

a dog play dominoes afore". "There's nowt clivvor aboot that dog son," says the shepherd, "it hasn't won a game yet."

51 Geordie Gets The Brush Off

There was a knock on Geordie's door one day, standing on the step was a brush salesman. "Good morning sir," he says. "Would your good lady like any brushes?" "Well ye've come on a bad day son," says Geordie, "the wife's gone abroad for a fortnight, she's staying with her sister in Blyth." "Not to worry," says the salesman, "I'll leave three samples, the wife can have a look at them, I'll call back in three weeks." So he left a clothes brush, a sweeping brush and a hedgehog with a handle on (toilet brush). Three weeks to the day the salesman called back at Geordie's house. "Good morning," he said. "Did your wife like any of the samples I left?" "Why I'll be honest," says Geordie, "she liked that claes brush, she thinks that sweeping brush is clivor, but she cares nowt for that lavotary brush, she'd sooner have the paper."

52 One Thing at a Time

Geordie went to sign on at the dole. The dole clerk says, "I've got just the job for you, can you drive?" "I can anaal," says Geordie. "Well," says the clerk, "start tomorrow, driver/conductor on a corporation bus, that means you drive, also collect fares." Next day Geordie gets on the road with his double decker bus. Two o'clock in the afternoon the phone rings in the bus depot. Geordie's on the phone, "Can ye git oot here sharp to Porcy Street, the bus has gone through a shop window, broken glass aal ower." "Good God!" says the inspector on the other end, "How did that happen?" "I divvent knaa," says Geordie, "I was upstairs taking the fares at the time."

53 "If I Can Help Somebody"

The big strike was on, coal was hard to get. Geordie being a pitman, got his free load of coal tipped outside his house. His wife said, "Isn't it a shyem, when you think about, here we are with all the coal we need, and that old lady doon the raa hasn't got a fire and ne coal or sticks?" "Why didn't ye tell us woman?" says Geordie. On with his coat, down to the old lady's house, knocks at the door. When the old lady answered he said, "Is that right what wor lass tells me, ye've got ne coal, ne sticks, ne fire?" "Aye, that's right son," says the old lady, "I can't afford coal or sticks." "In that case," says Geordie, "can I borrow your bleezer, ye'll not be needing it?"

54 Merry Christmas

It was Christmas in the big department store, Santa was there with his bag of toys, taking 10p pieces from the bairns, and in return giving them a little toy to blow their fingers off. One little raggy barefoot girl said, "Please Santa, could I have a present for 10p?" Santa dived in his bag, gave her a doll's pram, a walkie-talkie doll, two bottles of champagne, 6 boxes of chocolates and a big hamper of groceries. "Thank you Santa," lisped the little girl. "Do I get all these for 10p?" "Yes dear," says Santa, "and don't forget to tell your mother to have my supper ready when I get home."

55 A Visit to Rome

Geordie had a fortnight at Blackpool. When he was there he bought a lot of little Catholic trinkets, and when he was back home he was flashing them in the club, kidding his mates he'd been to Rome. One chap says, "What was Rome like Geordie?" "Smashing," says Geordie, "something like Amble withoot chip shops." "Did you see the Vatican?" says another lad. "I seen it ivvery day," says Geordie, "I used te gaan there to put a bet on." The club steward chipped in, "Did you see the Pope, Geordie?" "See him!" says Geordie, "I had me tea with him, he's a smashing bloke, ne swank or nowt, and his missis is a canny lass as weel."

56 A Dole-ful Tale

So Geordie was back on the dole, he went one day to draw his dole. The dole clerk says, "Sorry sir, there's no dole for you." "How's that?" says Geordie. "There's no stamps on your card sir," says the clerk. When Geordie got home he said to his wife, "Maggie there's ne dole, ne stamps on the card." "Divvent worry," she says, "I'll fettle that." So she fills the card with green shield stamps. Next day Geordie goes to the dole, hoys his card on the counter, the dole clerk looked at it. "That's better," he said. He went in the back and came back with an aluminium kettle, which he gave to Geordie.

57 Oh Mein Papa

Young Tadger came in from work one day, said to his father, "Fethor, I'd like to get married". "Oh aye," says his father, "who do you intend to marry?" "Why," says Tadger, "Sadie Robson!" "Ye divvent mean Sadie Robson from Woodbine Terrace? Cos ye canna marry hor son, ye see when I was a lad, I got about a bit, and that lass is yor sister and my dowter." A fortnight later Tadger approached his father

27

again, with a view to getting married. "Whe is it this time?" says the old man. "Jenny Simpson," says Tadger. "I told ye afore," says his father, "I got aboot when I was young, that lass is yor sister and my dowter." When Tadger's mother came in from shopping, her son's sitting crying. When she asked him why, he told her the whole story, how twice his father had refused him and why. "Take ne heed of him son," she says, "he's not yor father anyhoo."

58 Beauty is Skin Deep

It was Geordie's 25th wedding anniversary. When he came downstairs into the kitchen his wife Maggie says, "Geordie Pet, I'm wearing something today I've never worn for 25 years, can you guess what it is?" Geordie looked at her, "It's yor ganzie," he says. "No," she says, "it's not me ganzie." "I knaa," he says, "it's yor wellies." "No, wrang again," says Maggie. "Why," Geordie says, "it must be yor earrings." "No," says Maggie. "Why I give in," says Geordie, "what is it?" "I'll tell ye," says his wife, "it's me gas mask!"

59 Drop of Scotch

The Wooler bus was at the Haymarket, a big Scotsman got on, kilt, sporran, bag-pipes, the lot and a big carpet bag, which he placed on the luggage rack. The bus was so full, that it was on the Lion Bridge at Alnwick before the conductor got to the Scotsman. For his fare the Scotsman said, "A threepenny one to Wooler." "Ye must be joking," says the conductor, "ye got on at the Haymarket, the fare to Wooler is 56p." "I'm no giving ye 56p," says the Scot, "there's 3p, tak it or leave it!" The conductor stopped the bus on the bridge. "Off you get Jock," he says, "and there's your bag," and he threw the carpet bag out of the bus. Well it went clean over the bridge into the river Aln. As the bus moved off the Scotsman's standing on the bridge shaking his fist and shouting, "I'll hae ye prosecuted ye Sassenach! You're no satisfied wi cheating me oot o' ma fare, ye're trying to droon my wee boy!"

60 The Volunteer Organist

There was confusion in the club on Saturday night. The concert chairman got on the stage, "Ladies and Gentlemen! The organist hasn't turned up, is there anyone in the audience who can oblige?" A raggy unshaven old man hobbled up to the organ, sat down at the organ, and when he played it was sheer magic. No matter what anyone sang he accompanied them perfectly. Geordie sat watching him and noticed his shirt tail was hanging oot. Feeling sorry, he went to the old man, whispered in his ear, "D'ye knaa yor shart tails hingin oot?" "Why I've nivvor hord it hinney," says the old man, "but just ye kick off, I'll follow ye."

61 Say Nowt

Talking about Yanks - This American was passing the crematorium, he stopped a Geordie and said, "Tell me bud, what's that lil ol place over there?" "Why that's the crematorium," says Geordie. "Never heard of one of them," says the Yank, "reckon I could go in there and have a look around?" "I divvent see why not," says Geordie, "providing ye take your hat off and say nowt!" "Gee thanks," says the Yank. Five minutes later he came rolling down the steps. Geordie ran back, picked him up, dusted him down, and says, "What went wrang lad?" "Gee!" says the Yank, "I did just like you said. Took off mah hat, walks in, minding mah own business, when ah gits in what do ah see a lot of folk a-weepin and a-prayin, all ah did was ah said, Hi-ya folks, what's cookin?"

62 Shopping Today

Mind, ye can get owt in these big stores nooadays, can't ye? I was in Marks an' Spencer's the other day when a bashful young fellow came in. He says to the shopwaaker, "I'm supposed to be buyin' someick, an' I canna remember whether it's a casserole or a camisole." "That's easily settled son," the shopwaaker says, "is the bird deid or alive?"

A thought - An Optimist - A bloke that gets married at the age of ninety-three and buys a new hoose near a school.

63 Our Police are Wonderful

I was watching a football match between Newcastle Police and Gateshead Police, big 18 stone men kicking the ball around - fantastic. A little chap in front of me kept jumping up and down shouting, "Gan on! Knock his block off! Kick his heed in! Masacree him! Paralyze him!" I says, "Look sir, why divvent ye sit doon? I can't see the game for ye! Knock whose heed off, paralyze who?" "Any of them," he says, "they're all pollis's."

64 What Is a Geordie?

What is a Geordie? I've heard many people ask,
To give a definition is not an easy task.
Some think he's a heathen, who grows leeks and lives on beer
But if you listen for a while I'll give you my idea.

When God first made the Universe, His handiwork was grand,
He made a man of every creed, to cultivate each land.
He made Eskimos for Iceland, Africans to stand the heat,
But when it came to Geordieland, He say's I doot I'm beat.

So He made a man of iron, with muscles of forged steel,
For hewing coal and building ships, a job that He's done weel.
And just to finish off His job, at least so I've been told,
He completed His first Geordie, by giving him a heart of gold.

So when you ask, what is a Geordie? Just stop and think again,
If it wasn't for Geordie Stivinson, we'd've had ne railway train.
And aald Joe Swan from Sunderland, first made electric light,
And St. George slew the dragon, I'm varny sure that's right.

So d'ye wonder that I'm proud to be a Geordie lad,
A forst class team, the world's best beer, surely that can't be bad.
And when my earthly days are done, and I leave this world of sin,
I'd like to hear St.Peter say, 'Howay Geordie it's yor torn to get them in'.

65 Band Call

Geordie and Tucker were listening to the brass band in the park. Geordie says, "I knaa that tune, it's the overture from Lohengrin by Strauss." "Divvent be daft," says Tucker, "it's the concerto from Iolanthe by Beethoven!" As the argument waxed, Geordie says, "I'll just nip to the back, and have a look at the board". He came back, "Were both wrang Tucker," he says, "it's the refrain from Spitting by Order."

66 Keeping It In The Family

I was having a drink in the Earl Grey, two fellows next to me. One says to the other, "I seem to recognise yor fyce son, what's yor name?" The second one says, "They caal me Sammy Broon." "Why hev a pint," says the first one, "they caal me Joe Broon, where d'ye live son?" "I live in Theodosia Street," says the second. "Why I live there as weel," says the first man, "hev another pint. What number d'ye live?" "116," says the second man. "Why that's my hoose," says the first man, "hev a large whisky!" I called the manager over. "What's the matter with these two?" I asks him. "Oh take ne heed Dick," he says, "they're father and son, they've been on the beer for a month."

67 Diving Suit

Tucker entered his leeks in the Club Leek Show. When he got home his wife said, "How did you get on?" "Why," he says, "I won first prize, but I gave it away. It was nee good to me." "What was it?" she asked. "It was a diving suit," he says, "here's the ticket." She looked at the ticket, "Why ye daft gowk!" she says, "that's not a diving suit, it's a divan suite!"

68 The Milkmaid

Ha' ye seen the neet's paper? The price o' milk's gannin' up again. I see the government's got the matter in hand. The Minister of Agriculture's taakin' aboot takin' the bull by the horns. I think he's got the wrong animal by the wrang end.

Taakin' aboot cows, did I ivver tell ye aboot Lizzie Higginbottom? No, no, she's a milkmaid. That's a good job to get inte, but ye've got to have pull. Her father's a farmer. He's got a country place alang City Road. He taaks big. He was tellin' iz he farms five hundred acres an' keeps fifteen bulls. I says, "That's a lot o' bulls."

I went into the byre wi' Lizzie, to watch her milk a coo. That's an interestin' occupation - gannin' intiv a byre wi' Lizzie. A farmhand came rushin' up an' shooted, "Look oot, here comes a bull!" I jumped ower a five-foot waal, quiverin' wi' fright, but the lass nivver shifted off her stool. The bull hurtled up, then it quivered wi' fright an' aal an' slunk off with its tale between its legs. I peers ower the waal an' I says to the lass, "By gox, Lizzie, were ye not scared stiff?" "Not me," she says, "but mind, the bull was, this coo's his mother-in-laa!"

69 A New Stomach

Then take me brother-in-laa. Take him anywhere ye like. He was on holiday on a farm in the back o' beyond. He's aalways had trouble with his stomach. He had to diet. I divven' knaa what colour, but he had to dye it. No, he suffered from chills on the stomach - that's where his wife put her feet. Well, he was on this farm when he took bad. They were a lang way from medical help - the nearest vet was twelve miles away. Well, me brother-in-laa went tiv him with his stomach, there was ne point in leavin' it behind. The vet says, "There's nowt else for it, son, your stomach'll have to come oot. An' we're far from civilisation," he says. "We've got ne human stomach to replace it with. Nivver mind," he says, "the owld coo died this mornin. Waste not, want not." So they took oot me brother-in-laa's stomach an' put the coo's stomach in its place. Mind, I must say they made a first-class job of it, he's waakin aboot the day as fit as can be. Not only that - he's ganna calf in the spring.

70 Git Yor Hair Cut

The barbers shop was full. A fellow stuck his head round the door, looked around, says to the barber, "I'll come back later". Four times in one week he did this. The barber got suspicious, he says to the lather boy, "If that bloke comes tomorrow I want ye to follow him, see where he gans te." Sure enough on the Saturday morning the bloke comes, looks around, says, "Ye're full, I'll come back later". As soon as he left the lather boy went after him. When the lather boy came back the barber says, "Well son, where did he gan te?" "He went te yor hoose," says the boy.

71 Royal Appointment

The same barber shop was full, a fellow came in. "Could I have a haircut straighta- way?" he asked. "I'm sorry," says the barber, "ye can see the shop's full, ye'll hev te take your turn." "Why it's like this," says the chap, "I've got to be at Buckingham Palace in two hours time, the Queen is presenting me with a medal." The barber appealed to his customers, if they would object to this man getting served as it was a special occasion. They all agreed, so he got his haircut, and went away happy. A week later the same fellow came in the shop, wearing his medal. The barber says, "I see ye got yor medal, what's the Queen like?" She's smashing," says the bloke, far bonnier than her photos." "Did she speak to you?" said the barber. "She did anaal," says our friend. "She leaned over to pin my medal on, and just before she did she whispered in my ear, she said, 'Whe the hell cut yor hair like that?'"

72 The Lost Gord

It was a fine summer day, Geordie fancied a run out with his gord*. He set off from Byker, bowling his gord. When he got to Wideopen he decided to have a pint in Mary Gallon's pub. So he put his gord beside the window outside, laying his hook on the window sill. When he came oot his gord had gone. Geordie rang the police. When the police arrived he says, "Somebody pinched me gord while I was in the pub." "Well sir," said the pollis, "if you just give us particulars of the aforesaid gord if we come across anything we will get in touch with you." "That's all varry weel," says Geordie, "but how am I gan te git hyem?"

*Gord - iron hoop, propelled by hook.

73 Love Thy Neighbour

Billy Butlin, the holiday camp king, is in reality a very soft and kind hearted man. He once said to his manager at Filey Camp: "I want you to go to the local post office on pension day, grab the first old couple you see, don't let them argue, bung them in a taxi, bring them here, shove them in a chalet. We will give them a fortnights free holiday." The manager duly went down to the post office, selected the first old age couple he saw, gave them a free fortnight in a chalet. At the end of the fortnight he presented the two old folk on the stage. "Ladies and Gentlemen," he said, "we have given these two wonderful old folk a free holiday hoping it has brought a bit sunshine in their lives." Turning to the old man he said, "Have you enjoyed it sir?" "I hev anaal," said the old man, "the best holiday I've ivver had." "No questions?" he said. "No sir," says the old man. Then to the old lady, "Have you enjoyed it madam?" "Yes sir," she said. "Any questions?" "Only one sir," she said, "I'd like to know the name of the old gentleman?"

74 The Shoe's on the Other Foot

Geordie had had a night out with the boys. Next morning he was having difficulty in putting his pit boots on. His wife says, "Ye greet drunken lout, ye've got yor buyets on the wrang feet!" "Yor bloody reet," says Geordie, "they shud be on yours!"

75 The Labourer is Worthy of his Hire

Two old maids had a little corner shop which sold everything from groceries to patent medicines. One day a big young lad came into the shop. "Can you help me?" he said to the old maid behind the counter. "Every time I see a woman I get an uncontrollable passion, I want to grab her, hug her, kiss her. Can you give me anything for this?" "Just howld on son," she says, "I'll nip in the back and hev a word with me sister." Half an hour later she came back. "I've had a word with my sister," she says, "and we've decided to give you £10 a week and your full board!"

76 Talk of The Devil

Tucker's wife was getting fed up with his continual drinking, so she decided to give him a gliff. She knew he took a short cut home through the churchyard as he was a fearless man, in drink. So, on Saturday night, she hid behind a gravestone with a white sheet over her head. Sure enough at closing time Tucker came staggering through the churchyard singing Blaydon Races, palatic he was. As he got near the gravestone Jinnie jumped out and in deep voice said, "I'm the Divil, and I've come to claim my own!" Tucker looked at her and said, "Shake hands hinney, I married yor sister."

77 Thanks Yank

Two Yanks were walking down Percy Street, one said to the other, "Gee Hank ah shore is hungry". A little lad passing heard them and said, "Mister, there's a smashing pie shop doon the road, hot pies 5p each". "Gee son, that's great! There's 15p, bring mah buddy and me a pie and get one for yourself." Ten minutes later the laddie came back eating a hot pie, handed the yanks 10p. "There's your change mister," he says, "they only had one left."

78 Fire Away
There was a big fire in Ashington, the Bro's Finklestein Super Stores was gutted. After the fire the insurance man came to assess the damage. He questioned the first brother, Aby Finklestein, "What do you think caused the fire sir?" "Vell," said Aby, "It could have been von of the employees dropped a cigarette end." He then asked the second brother, Hymie, what he thought was the cause. "It could have been the boiler house door vas open and a bit of hot coal dropped out and started a blaze." The little offfice boy was standing by, "Please mister, I can tell ye what caused the fire." "Can ye son?" says the inspector, "What was it?" "It was the lights," says the laddie. "You mean the electric lights?" says the inspector. "No sir!" said the boy. "The Isrealites!"

79 Faith Can Increase Mountains
The faith healer visited Seghill. Dick Dodds who stammered and Steve Ridley who was a hunchback went to seek his advice. The faith healer told them, "When you go to bed tonight, say a prayer, sing a hymn and you will be cured." When next morning Dick woke up, lo and behold his stammer had gone. I'll away roond and see how Stevie's come on, he thinks. Stevie's wife answered the door, "He's still in bed and he'll not git up," she says. Dick gans upstairs, Stevie's under the bedclothes. "Stevie!" says Dick, "I'm cured, I divvent stammer any more. How are you?" Stevie's voice came from under the bedclothes, "I'll tell ye hoo I am, I said a prayer, I divvent knaa ne hymns, so I sang a chorus of the Desert Song. I've got two humps noo!"

80 Geordie Refusal
Geordie and family were on holiday in Italy. Little Tadger says, "Dad, can I have an ice cream from that cafe ower the road?" "Sartinly bonny lad," says Geordie. "There's the money son, git yersel a big un while you're on." Little Tadger came back crying. "Fethor!" he says, "I canna hev an ice cream, he refuses to serve Geordies." Geordie says, "What! I'll fettle him!" Over he goes to the cafe, says to the man behind the counter, "What's the idea, refusing to serve my laddie with ice cream?" "Sorry senor, the bosses orders, he says never serve Geordies with ice cream." "Where's the boss?" says Geordie. "In the office," says the man. Geordie goes in the office. The boss says, "Wot cheor? I'm from Jarra." "What?" says Geordie, "You're a fellow Geordie, why did ye refuse to serve my laddie with ice cream?" "Hold on!" says the boss. "I'll tell you why, hev ye tasted wor ice cream?"

81 A Poor Yolk

Geordie was passing a farm in the country, a notice outside said Fresh Farm Eggs. Geordie thought, "I'll buy a dozen for wor lass, she likes a fresh egg." When his wife broke the eggs they were empty shells. Geordie goes back to the farm next day and says to the farmer, "Them eggs I bowt for the wife were just empty shells, ne yolk, ne white". The farmer went and collected another dozen, broke them open. Sure enough they were empty as well. "That does it!" says the farmer. He goes down the hen house with his gun, lines all the hens against the wall, points the gun at them and says, "Now then, which one of you has been taking the pill?"

82 A Dying Wish

Jocker was in a bad way, in fact he thought he was on his way oot. He says to his wife, "Jennie if I snuff it, I divvent want ye te be lonely, ye're still an attractive woman, and if ye feel like getting married again, ye've got my blessing. But I want to ask ye one favour, if you de git married agyen, divvent let him wear my claes." "Divvent worry Jocker hinney," says his wife, "they divvent fit him anyway."

83 Blow The Wind Southerly

Geordie was made redundant, he got a job as a rent collector on the council. There was one old lady who would not pay her rent. Geordie was called into the office and told he was to serve an eviction order on this old lady, if he failed he would be sacked. Away he goes on his bike, the old lady was smarter than him, she saw him coming up the road, stuck a piece of cardboard over the back of the letter box. Geordie couldn't put it through the letter box, no luck, so he tried to put it under the door, but the old lady was on her knees with a pair of bellows, and every time Geordie shoved it under the door she blew it back. After a dozen attempts with no results he went back to the office. "Hev ye served the writ?" says his boss. "No I havn't," says Geordie, "and I'll tell ye this, if I lived in a draughty hoose like that I wouldn't pay my rent either!"

84 A Bare Living

Talking about graveyards, two skeletons met in the graveyard one night. One skeleton said to the other, "How are you? How long have you been dead?" "I'm not dead!" said the second skeleton. "I'm the curate!"

85 Wor Tricky Vicar

The vicar in wor church thowt he'd make things more interesting, he invited the congregation to write down any subject they fancied him preaching on, and place the papers on his pulpit. Tucker Johnson thowt he'd be clivvur, he wrote 'constipation' on an old Woodbine packet and placed it on the pulpit. But the vicar wasn't to be beat, on the Sunday, he went in the pulpit and said, "Brethren, the subject of my sermon today is constipation. I will commence by saying Moses went up unto the mountain, whereupon he took the tablets and wandered forth into the wilderness."

86 Thou Shalt Have A Good Memory
Talking about vicars. This vicar said to his verger, "James, I've had my bicycle stolen today, but I have a plan to regain it. On Sunday I will make my sermon The Ten Commandments, when I come to the commandment that says Thou Shalt not Steal, I shall pause, and the guilt will show on the culprit's face." But when Sunday came the vicar preached an entirely different sermon, never even mentioned the Commandments. After the service the verger said to the vicar, "Sir, I thought you were going to speak on the Ten Commandments?" "Well James, I was preparing my sermon last night, and when I came to the Commandment which said Thou Shalt not Commit Adultery, I remembered where I left my bicycle."

87 Pre-War (Price)
The Blacksmith's Arms was full of customers. This bloke goes to Peggy the barmaid, "Could I hev a pint of 1914 beer Miss?" he says. Peggy goes to the manager, "There's a nut case at the bar asking for a pint of 1914 beer, what should I do?" "Give him a pint of Scotch ale, he'll nivvor knaa the difference," said the manager. So Peggy fills a pint of Scotch, takes it to the stranger. "There you are sir, one pint of 1914 beer." "Thank you," says the bloke, "there's fourpence."

88 A Safe Bet
Old Miss Simpson was going down the High Street when she spotted a raggy old man standing on the corner-end. Feeling sorry for him she gave him a pound note saying, "Take Courage". Two days later, she was going down the High Street again, the same old man was there. He came over to her and pressed eleven pound notes in her hands. "What's this?" she said. "Take Courage lady," he said, "came up ten to one."

89 There's Safety In Numbers
Geordie moved into a new house and the staircase needed papering badly. So he went to the chap next door, "Can you help me mate, I've just moved in next door, can you tell me how many rolls of wallpaper you got for your staircase?" "Sartinly,"

says his neighbour, "I got ten rolls." "Thanks mate," says Geordie. A week later Geordie knocks at his neighbour's door again. "I got ten rolls like you said, I've papered my staircase and I've got two rolls left!" "That's funny," says his neighbour, "so have I."

90 Geordie at the Hoppings
Geordie went to the Hoppings, on the Town Moor at Race Week. He took his dog in the flea circus, the dog stole the show. In fact, it ran away with the leading lady.

Geordie was passing a gipsy's caravan, (she was a fortune teller - Madame Zaza). She grabbed Geordie, dragged him into her caravan and gazed into her crystal ball. She looked at Geordie and said, "Someone very near to you is very worried about money." "It'll be ye hinney," says Geordie, "I've come oot wi nowt."

91 Till Death Us Do Part
Mind, what a craze this bingo is. I mind when they made the Westgate pictur-hoose intiv a bingo. One rainy day a queue of women was waiting ootside in the rain - to worship the Great God Bingo. A funeral passed, one lady stepped out of the queue, placed a rose on the hearse and stepped back in the queue. The lady next to her says, "By it's nice to meet somebody like you in these hard days with a bit of understanding and sympathy." "Why it's the least I could do hinney," said the first woman, "after all, he was a good man to me."

92 Coonciloor Ramsey
Take my mate Jimmy Ramsey (please). He's been on the dole that long he goes to the staff dances. Well, he was elected to the Coxlodge Club Committee, he bowt property, he was made secretary, he got a Rolls Royce, finally he was made a councillor. On his first night as a councillor he was celebrating at the club, his mates were clapping him on the back, buying him drinks. "Good cld Jim," they were saying. "Not so much of the Jim," he says, "Coonciloor Ramsey from now on, and divvent forget it!" Two o'clock in the morning he arrives home - palatic, hangs his clothes in the wardrobe. Their lass is lying in bed, he looks at her and says, "Move ower for Coonciloor Ramsey!" "Why ye'll hev te be sharp hinney," she says, "wor Jimmy'll be in shortly."

93 Look After Yersel
It was the first night they'd played bingo in Hazelrigg Club. Two old miners sitting next to each other, the caller shouts, "All the sixes, clickety click!" "Gan on," says old Tom to Sam, "yeh've got that." The caller shouts, "Legs eleven!" "Gan on," says

Tom, "ye've got that an aal." "Two little ducks!" says the caller, "All the 2's!" "Ye've got that one Sam," says Tom. "Haald yor gob, Tom," says old Sam, "mark yer own card man, leave me to mine!" "Oh that's alreet," says Tom, "mines been full for the last ten minutes."

94 An Amateur
I got taalking to one of the cowboy stars one neet. He was telling me aboot the strong men they hev in America. He says, "Bud, I gotta cousin in Oklahoma by the name of Clancy. He drives a railroad engine 2 miles long, half-a-mile wide. He pulls up at the Colorado Railroad depot, picks the engine up in his right hand, oils the wheels with the left, and puts the whole caboodle back on the rails. How's that for strength?" "By Gods," I says, "that's clivor, but I've got a brother in Wallsend called Jake - chews hammers!" "Gee," says the Yank, "that guy must be a professional!" "No," I tells him, "just a hammerchewer!"

95 Hearse to the Next Time
When I was a lad there was two undertakers in Gosforth, Harry Robson and Mick Hall. In those days the hearse was drawn by horses with plumes on their heads. Then came the great day Harry Robson was the first one in Gosforth to get a motor hearse. That night Harry and Mick met in the Earl Grey. Over a pint, Mick says to Harry, "Well Harry, how's the new motor hearse gannin?" "Ye'll not believe this," says Harry, "but ivverybody in Gosforth is dying for a ride in it."

96 A Weighty Problem
I mind the old dole in New Bridge Street, a wooden hut with partitions, where you signed on. The pencils were tied on a length of string to prevent anyone pinching them. Geordie went to sign on one day, the pencil had no point on, so Geordie shouted to one of the dole clerks, "This pencil will not write!" he says. "Put your weight on man," says the dole clerk. So Geordie promptly put down 'ten stone seven'.

97 Live and Let Live
I think my mate Tucker's gannin barmy. When I caaled for him the day, he was weshin the dishes. "Mind, you're a mug," I says. "I wouldn't de that for ne woman." "Why Dick hinney, ye've got te give and take," he says. "after aal wor lass helps me te make the beds." I'd hev thumped his lugs, if I hadn't hev been pushing the pram with me pinney on at the time.

98 The Housing Problem

Three Geordie lads were in court, on a charge of drunk and disorderly conduct. "Where do you live?" said the judge to the first man. "365 Scotswood Road," says the man. To the second man he said the same thing. "No fixed abode yor honor." And the third man says, "I've got a room off him."

99 Geordie Weshington

Sep Walker was varry proud of his netty doon at the bottom of the garden, with the burn running past it. Till one sad day Sep's netty was pushed into the burn. The irate Sep grabbed his son Tucker. "Listen lad," he says, "did ye push that netty in the burn?" "No fethor," says young Tucker, "I didn't!" "Sit doon son," says Sep, "I'll tell ye a story. Once upon a time there was a lad caaled Geordie Weshington and he chopped his fethor's cherry tree doon. When his fethor got in from back shift he says to young Geordie, 'Did ye chop that cherry tree doon?' 'Why fethor,' says young Geordie, 'I canna tell a lie, yes I chopped the cherry tree doon.' So instead of giving him a good belting, his fethor forgave him cos he'd told the truth. Noo I'll ask you again, did ye or did ye not push that netty in the burn?" "Fethor," says young Tucker, "after hearing that story I've got te tell the truth, I pushed the netty in the burn." Why Sep picks him up, lays him ower his knee, took off his belt and gave young Tucker the biggest howking he'd ivor had. Tucker's blairing his eyes oot, "Fethor! Why did you giv iz a hiding, when I told ye the truth? Geordie Weshington's fethor forgave him when he told the truth aboot the cherry tree." "Aye I knaa," says Sep, "but Geordie Weshington's fethor wasn't sitting in the cherry tree at the time."

100 The Geordie Netty

I had a canny job during the war, I wez an air-raid warden gannin roond the colliery raas, lookin for chinks and japs in windows with me little flash-lamp. Why one neet I sees a little light in a little window. I knocked on the door and a little voice says, "Who's there?" "Send yor muthor oot!" I sez. "I canna, me mothor went oot when me fethor came in," said the little voice. "Why send yor fethor oot!" I sez. "Me fethor went oot when me brother came in." "Why I'll hev a word with yor brother!" The little voice replied, "Me brother went oot when me sister came in." "Alreet," I says, "I'll hev a word with your sister!" "No," said the little voice, "ye canna de that, ye see me sister went oot when I came in." "By gox," I says, "what a funny hoose this is!" "This is not a hoose mistor," says the little voice, "this is the netty!"